The Racial Justice Series
By
Roberto Schiraldi

~

Healing Love Poems
for white supremacy culture:
Living Our Values

Unexpurgated*Racial Justice Poetry
with Healing Meditations

Men and Racism:
The Healing Path

Multicultural Counseling
with Boys and Men:
A Healing Guide

Post Traumatic Macho Disorder
The Way Home

POST TRAUMATIC MACHO DISORDER:
The Way Home

The Greatest Threat To Our Planet
Awakening From The Nightmare

ROBERTO SCHIRALDI

BALBOA.PRESS

A DIVISION OF HAY HOUSE

Balboa Press books may be ordered through booksellers or by contacting:

Balboa Press
A Division of Hay House
1663 Liberty Drive
Bloomington, IN 47403
www.balboapress.com
844-682-1282

Print information available on the last page.

ISBN: 979-8-7652-5784-5 (sc)
ISBN: 979-8-7652-5783-8 (hc)
ISBN: 979-8-7652-5782-1 (e)

Library of Congress Control Number: 2024925170

Balboa Press rev. date: 11/27/2024

Contents

Loving Dedication

To You My Precious Love Eileen
For Helping Me Feel Safe Enough
To Be A Lot Less Macho
And A Lot More
My Authentic Gentle Loving Self

Loving Gratitude

Huge thank you, my brother Glenn for your commitment
To healing our world through Love.
And for your important and inspiring
Post Traumatic Stress Disorder Sourcebook

I whole heartedly believe that the underlying
Source of most of our traumatic stress lies
Within this all-pervasive dis-ease of Macho-ism.

Mostly..thank you for your Love.

Prelude One

Most of the havoc on this planet
is perpetrated by little boys
wearing big man costumes.

Prelude Two

Nothing is so strong as gentleness
Nothing so gentle as real strength

Indigenous Wisdom

Introduction

Hi,

Welcome...and thank you for opening this book.

So why did I write it, and why call it <u>Post Traumatic Macho Disorder</u>?

<u>First</u>......because we live in a world...which...while it is filled with all kinds of beauty......is also often....crazy...... dangerous... and sick.

<u>Second</u>.....whenever I've acted all macho....it's never, ever felt right.....and I know it disrespected me..and the other.

And <u>Third</u>.....I need to get this out of me.........the hurt...the frustration...the rage...at this blight of macho-ism...on our selves and our world...and make a positive contribution to addressing it.

~

While I'm not the smartest apple on the tree....I do know one thing for sure.....this macho stuff....is not only a great obstacle to our most happy and healthy.....thriving existence......it is also ..... literally ....killing us!!!

<u>**Macho-ism can pervade, and effect every aspect of our lives....and the lives of everyone else... and everything else... on this planet.**</u>

First, so we're clear,...some definitions of macho (from the American Dictionary), are "<u>super strong and powerful, forceful, hyper sexual, showing no emotion /determined to not show weakness (or vulnerability), more on this later),...."He's too macho to admit he was hurt by his girlfriend leaving him"....or..."too macho to admit a woman can do a job as well as he can.</u>" These are just a couple of examples of the dehumanization of us men...which hurts us..and all others in our lives.....and prevents us from being our best, most loving selves.

Please know...I'm not saying any of this to disrespect, insult, degrade or put down anyone. For sure, life can be challenging to say the least, and does throw a lot of curves our way. I firmly believe we each are doing the best we can at any moment....given where we come from, and what we've learned and had modeled for us. I only want to offer support here, so we can better understand how being macho hurts us......to explore better alternatives for improving our lives, if we want that, and perhaps.... even making it a little easier, and more enjoyable.

~

To repeat....I see macho mentality as degrading to each of us....and as the main threat to our well-being ....and to the well-being of our children, and our childrens' children, and on and on...for as long as it continues...or til we finally succeed in destroying our planet.

~

Don't want to come off as harsh and judgemental........as I'm certainly no better or worse than anyone else.........and....... am definitely very frustrated and angry at how this macho-ism has hurt me... and our world........

I'm sick of all this macho stuff....<u>inside me</u> ....and so many of us.....Since the Beginning. It's all a front...a sham...a lie..... it's not who we really are....we just learned it ....and use it... to try and feel a little better about ourselves.

There are many obviously traumatic stressful events, such as sexual assault, murder, suicide,..... as well as chronic traumatic stressors such as racism, sexism, homophobia.

<u>**Macho-ism is less obvious.....yet nonetheless can be even more horrific, devastating, and lethal...... especially since it is such a universally habitual and accepted value .....that often.... if not usually..... goes unchallenged due to........**</u>

<u>…..FEAR…….Of Those In Power!</u>

<u>We live in a culture of FEAR….with repeated threats of war, violence, sexual assault, poverty, physical/dis-ease, environmental, emotional, social, spiritual, economic insecurity, racism, sexism, homophobia, classism, xenophobia……and on and on.</u>

And this <u>**macho behavior / habit (or addiction)**</u> can take many different forms…..

physically (needing to prove I'm stronger, tougher than), mentally (needing to prove I'm smarter than), emotionally (needing to prove I'm more "sane" than… being detached, less emotional (yet, of course, anger is allowed in men).

Each of these forms…..pits us against one another.

And while it has it's main origins in us men………..and predominantly still lies …within us…. **let's not make any mistake here……………**

<u>…………*macho is no respecter of gender*…..*or* *sexual orientation, class etc.,.* (Women…… Everyone)</u>……<u>can be all macho too</u>… as we all want to feel good about our selves… and we all want… and of course… <u>deserve</u>.. to be treated "<u>right</u>", and <u>deserve</u> an

"equitable" piece of the pie..etc......and that deserves a whole other book, perhaps many books).

And "Post Traumatic Disorder"....because it surely is traumatizing to ourselves and all the rest of the planet....and it is "post"...since it is a constant...**repeat trauma / assault on our natural desire for peace** and gentleness...and we sure are born into,....a "certifiable", on-going..."Disorder"....as often our outer world...as well as our inner world... are both waaaay dis-ordered, confused, mixed up, topsy turvey, …....making it extremely difficult to savor all the beauty and goodness. As Anne Wilson Shaef spoke of in her book 'When Society Becomes the Addict', addicts are the scapegoats for an addicted society." So before we so freely label or diagnose ourselves or others with the term "disorder", I think we need to look a lot more carefully at the culture/s we live in.

I think macho also qualifies as a dangerous...."disease".....since it is definitely....chronic, contagious, debilitating, life-threatening, …...effecting every part of our health......physically, emotionally, mentally, socially, spiritually.

So... being macho sure doesn't help with being healthy and happy. And, definitely causes and exacerbates most of our problems.

However, **<u>the alternatives to macho...are relieving...and life-enhancing... remedies to our often sick world</u>**. So we'll continue to explore them.

And why *'The Way Home'*?

Because it certainly looks like... we've lost our way. Maybe, really, since day one. Because we've allowed this plague to go unaddressed, seeing it as...maybe "natural"..."boys just being boys"... …..or …."they're just being <u>protective</u>"(or are they really getting off on being the "boss" and being controlling?)..... For sure in our highly mechanized world, we've gotten "distracted" by loud, quick fixes and mis-guided values, rather than listening to the still little voice of truth ...home..inside us, which always re-minds us...who we are and how to be our most loving selves. But that seems to be a "radical" concept...that we have what we need inside...rather than living by the quest to "accumulate" things outside of ourselves. Much more on this follows.

So again.....the <u>Source</u> of all the the sickness inside us and our world, as I see it, is **rooted in macho poison.**

This insulting, **<u>cancerous dis-ease</u>** of macho-ism...... …......clutters up all the beauty.....all the Love.... that lives inside each of us...and which is our truest....healthiest self.

Ahh...the "balance". Wise ones have always taught us that..."the darkness can help us appreciate the light, and vice versa.".....**And.**.....**we have a choice**....always....a choice who I am ...and who do I choose to Be...in this moment... and this moment....and this moment.

More on balance to come.

The good news!......All the toxic, debilitating, life threatening "isms"....racism....sexism.....homophobia....classism..... xenophobia.....and on and on.....that so diminish each of us.....can be healed when we expose the macho which lives inside each of us.

So basically flip it...**the reasons we act all macho.... can actually be our teachers... our guides...
for healing ourselves and our world. When we figure out what we *Really* need to help us feel....safe, secure, whole, worthy, comforted, nurtured, accepted, appreciated, respected, cared for, then we can stop the insulting (to ourselves and others) macho front, and safely return home to our most beautiful *authentic* selves.**

~

Again, basically, to further simplify.....**the "source"...the antidotes for our healing....as I see it..... *lies within....* for example...the macho man little boy ....*who is really***

looking for some tenderness....in a tough, dog eat dog world....but doesn't know how to get it.

I work with men who have been traumatized...in early childhood...many for most of their lives. And **one main thing we all share in common...is the great challenge......of the excruciatingly painful concept of ...._being tender, gentle, kind with ourselves..._ _(because we weren't taught that early on as little boys)._ This is a brutal and life threatening problem....for so many of us.**

Yep....I can hear many of you reacting to that statement with...Bull!!! I don't need any tenderness! …........we'll leave that here for now...and tend to it in a little bit.

~

Being willing to choose to be humble enough and brave enough....the balance again.....to explore this topic ..... uncovering ...and healing …........the macho part of us..... can lead us to have more loving happy and fulfilling lives. That's why I wrote this book.

I'm gonna free flow.....and do my best to not plan it out so ultra carefully.....yet.....keep choosing to be "vulnerable" ...and see what comes up.

We can each choose to keep the "safety harness" on....that is strangling us.....and keeping us imprisoned in our macho suit of armor. Or maybe choose to loosen it, or even take it off.

It's up to each of us to choose. And I get it...no one can force us......it's got to be up to each of us to choose....<u>when we are ready....to choose a better way</u>!

And since you chose to open this book....my guess is...at least some part of you is ready.

This is a very personal book for me... that goes to the "heart" of the macho....and offers a healing path for the future. While you will likely find some of this to be troubling...I trust that you will find most of it to be supportive, encouraging, and comforting.

So I invite us each now.....to take a deep, comforting, life giving breath......maybe shake it out a little.........maybe even smile a little.......and perhaps be willing to take a little walk together....down this winding trail...which I'm confident that you will also find to be... empowering, refreshing, freeing, and life-affirming!

Thank You again...... for being brave enough... and caring enough... to give it a try.

In Support Of Our Loving World,

Roberto

To begin with, I've chosen to add some poems from my previous books that hit "home" for me...and hopefully for you too. I know that poetry is not usually seen as macho.....I started writing poems to help me keep somewhat sane during my time in the service during the Vietnam War.

We Men. This Man

Since the beginning of time
we men have tried,
to be in charge,
while many have died.

We thought it our duty
our right, our job,
to run the show,
and even to rob

others of their rights,
a negative effect
preventing so many
of freedom and respect

If we're in control
have the power and the toys

we think we're men
but really only boys.

For the values often taught
can fool us into thinkin
that the answer lies outside us,

like money, and like drinkin.....

Then finally one day,
we awaken from the haze,
and we realize we've been duped,
not been our finest days.

And hopefully what we get,
is the wisdom from above,
That what we've always needed.....
is a heart that's filled with love.

FRS/10/2/19

Macho Man...From boyhood to man.

The refusal to succumb
renders us all numb
from **feeling** who we are
alienated from ourselves... so far.

From the time we're a child
we're taught to be wild
or intellectual, number one
is what we're molded, to be fun

To prove our worth, the stronger,
a crybaby no longer.
Tender feeling is to be weak
walled off from gentle
is what we seek.

To always be at the top
Otherwise we're a flop.
Competing with each other,
instead of each our brother.

Sets us up to fight and pretend
we're in control until the end...
over women, animals, the land
no clear picture of healthy man.

All others perceived as a threat
don't let them see us sweat.
Racism, sexism, homophobia,
refugees, cleansing utopia ("udopeya").

What a treacherous, treacherous game,
It's important to finally name.
For we'll never be truly alive
staying stuck in this race to survive.

And if we really want to be free,
we've got to take off the blinders to see
that we've been hoodwinked all along
and being macho is all wrong.

It's a front, a lie, a sham,
Being gentle and kind's who I am
Being brave and honest and humble
Admitting I'm wrong when I stumble.

Committed to equity for all
prevents me from the "great fall"
from being all I can be
loving human...like you and me.

Being nurturing, considerate and kind
we're finally out of the bind

Then we wake up
and shout with joy

As we cull the man
from the boy.
And we know that fully living
is to share, and to be giving.

Each one, our sister, our brother
love inside for our self and each other,
giving love to ourselves and each other
giving love to ourselves and each other.

12/31/19

Macho "Values"/ The Origins Of Machoism

<u>Power, Wealth, Control.</u>

I'm gonna start with these three "kissin cousins".....as they are the "heart" ... of what I see as the ultimate demise of us all.

<u>Power</u>...

…..........over what....who....when....where????.......

…..since the beginning....we men have "fought" to <u>prove</u> ourselves "worthy"...by demonstrating our "power" over …..every thing...and every one.

In the caves....exerting power over women....casting them out of the caves during menstruation....and when giving birth......why?..........can you say....insecurity.......fear....(please see a most amazing book by Wolfgang Lederer, '<u>**The Fear Of Women**</u>')....... jealousy...... ....the blood...evil spirits...... women can create life.....the great mystery of life...(we can plant our seed)......

….power over other men....animals..........the land......

why?.......for sure... for survival...so that part makes sense..... at least with others.....with the animals and the land .

So we used to build monuments to our penis....and tried to prove who had the biggest....

hmm…......still doing both........still doing both......

And we created suits of armor for protection.......especially for our most "vulnerable" parts. For, as any one of us men, who has been kicked between the legs knows....we are very "vulnerable".... There's the ticket...."vulnerable"........**vulnerable.....and the <u>fear</u> that goes with that.......can't ever let down my guard and be vulnerable....because the world is not a safe place........how could it be....when fear of being vulnerable is so running rampant. So I think we could make a good argument for "fear of being vulnerable" as one of the most powerful values that "governs" our decision making.......and therefore.....our world. Bigger...better...bigger homes....bigger cars....more weapons....more....more ...more...and finally we'll be safe... and secure.......at least until we feel threatened.......and then all hell brakes loose.**

So a balance pause here. Ahh. Breathing.....

Nothing wrong with fear...and wanting to feel safe and protected.....and protective ...of our loved ones. However............However..........I have learned ….over this lifetime.....and perhaps....many, many …...lifetimes....... that the only thing and person I really have any power

over.....or better to say ...with..........is..... guess who????
I know you know this.......yep.............

<u>me</u>......(or you, yourself). For I can always choose how I
treat me....and I can choose to improve that...and how I
treat others.......and that takes all I have.....

And sometimes I'm very good at how I treat me (and
others)...and sometimes... I out and out ...suck at it.
So ....great secret here.....if I tend to my business....of
how I treat me....and others.......I'll never be bored.....
and I will continue to grow and continue to be more
and more healthy and happy. Again a huge life goal....
and one, which we unfortunately are not usually given
a lot of training in........thus one of the most important
reasons for offering this little book.

.......and that "fear" is simply the universe's way of asking
me...."what would love do now?"......what <u>loving action</u> is
needed to address whatever I'm feeling afraid of. The
traditional knee jerk reaction is either "fight or flight".
And of course sometimes that is what is needed. However,
we are not usually facing dinosaurs everyday.........although
we can sure make it feel that way....if we are seeing every
thing and everybody as threats....especially if we see them
as "different,".. "not from here,".. "Gay", etc.

So where does this threat mentality come from?

<u>**Wealth....**</u>

<u>**…............Money.....Material Stuff.........**</u>

<u>**…............or lack thereof....or fear of losing what we have.......**</u>

~ ~ ~

<u>**…..or........**</u>

<u>**Real Wealth......**</u>

<u>**Real Wealth... Worth.... Worthy**</u>
…......As my very wise and loving brother Glenn taught me in his workbooks on Self esteem and Resilience....... we are each born a "crystal".....crystal being.....worthy.... exactly how we are....valuable......important.....worthy of Love, acceptance, respect....dignity......not needing to be earned or proven........it just is.

And yet, that is often not the message we get.....actually usually just the opposite......that our sense of worth has to be continuously earned, proven....by accomplishing goals, accumulating materials, money, etc..... (not that there's anything wrong with goals, and materials and money)......

but that is not what determines our worth......and those things that lie outside ourselves...like <u>money and material things</u> create a "tenuous" hold on our sense of "ok"ness, and "safety" and "security"....take them away ...and ...who are we?............the question is does that ok-ness, safety and security lie inside us?.........and we don't have to act "tough" to impress anyone...to continually prove anything.. to anybody or ourselves.....we don't have to "act" at all because we feel "secure" within ...Being our "authentic" self. (Bullies are most often scared little boys (or girls),who need to scare others to feel better about themselves). And that tough guy persona / suit of armor/emotional distance/ keeps us ...disconnected ...."alienated" from ourselves and others (more on this later). This is one of the key reasons so many men are so miserable, discontented, and mean spirited........

…...........our worth is like the crystal....always there...... even if we get mud on top.......once we "clean" ourselves"…. we return to our natural worthy self.....If we are smart enough and humble enough....and brave enough.... to repeatedly re-member that truth.....and continually claim it.....by repeatedly <u>choosing</u> ...with every thought, word and deed....to live our lives in harmony with our highest core values. (please see the All Life Is Sacred Proposal and the Values Inventories towards the end of this book).

Worth

Each of us is born worthy.
That worth lives inside us.
It's who we are.

If we're not taught it,
It's up to us to choose it.
This road ain't easy.

Self-Worth
The Core Self
Sacred

The Beautiful Crystal
is the image
of the
core self,

sacred...

worthwhile,
worthy of love,
valuable,
precious,
born this way.

Doesn't have to be **earned...**

This is our essence.....

rather than externals ….
like goals,
achievement,
others' approval,
wealth,
being #1,
success.

There may be
mud on the crystal....
but when I clean it off.....
the crystal remains....
worthwhile
beautiful,
worthy of love.

Teaching our parents
that This
is the most important message
to give their young ones...

"I love you unconditionally....
and no matter what you do or accomplish,
that's all gravy.......

I love you for Being Alive
I love you for Being You"

This is why so many
are suicidal,
because they truly believe
they can never do enough
or Be enough
to earn
their parents love.

And if worth
is judged
by color of skin,
race,
nationality,
gender,
sexual orientation,
disability,
economic status,
and other considerations......
this is a huge obstacle
to ever feeling
fully acceptable
and worthwhile.

I choose
to Believe
in my core worth......
and all others'...
and all life's core worth....
all life is sacred....
and we are all connected,

and all one....

let it be so....

This
is what I choose
to believe.

Hope you do...too.

If this is what we taught and lived by.....our parents, teachers, churches, police, military, bosses.... presidents....government....all of our institutions....all of us....

....racism.....and all the other "isms'....would be a dead issue.

~

Living by our belief in, and our commitment to... our innate worth.........is the secret to a happy, healthy.... Love-filled life.

Again... this is what our highest and most important teachings need to reflect....in families, our schools, our churches, ...our businesses, our governments.........in every part of our lives....our collective world. It clearly is not how many of our lives, our government and our world conduct business. And we wonder why things get so messed up ...seemingly.....so easily....and the beat goes on....and on...and on.....bouncing up and down...side to side...........

On a related note.…..can you say.......huge fear and insecurity around the elections....because we have such little confidence in our leaders.....especially with all the macho bravado in the debates and campaign promos, which are often so self degrading,...... with the posturing, criticizing, insulting....like two infantile bullies in a school yard......and <u>such very, very poor examples for our young ones</u>.......///and especially since the values that run things are sooooo flimsy....have been since the beginning......

...we've never made things right.....really being honest about the lies.....and we wonder why we don't have trust.....<u>we can only have trust...when we acknowledge</u>

<u>**when we screw up.....and then make it right by those we've hurt.......a most basic way to live life.......since the beginning.**</u>

<u>***People who are "truly" strong inside...are most often humble...and willing to acknowledge their flaws, and are honest.....so don't feel the need to put on some false image to prove how tough they are.***</u>

Back to the Macho Values

And <u>control</u>.....

….....................I...(we) ...can really only have power and control....over one being.....and that is …..me..... (us). I know....that each of us knows this really basic truth.....that I know this......and you know this.....it's just that most of us aren't taught this....and it's not really mentioned very often....and so easy to forget......as the world doesn't seem to function with that truth.

As Victor Frankel writes (in his inspirational book 'Man's Search for Meaning', about his experience facing imminent death in a Nazi Concentration Camp), all we really have any control over....is our "attitude".

No one can control that, but us.

So we can choose to have an <u>attitude of gratitude</u>. Clearly...not an easy choice in the midst of so much stuff that doesn't feel safe and affirming. And yet, very, very <u>empowering to know..and to live our lives with this conviction.</u>

<u>**Abundance.**</u> **Now there's a word...a concept. Do I really believe that I live with abundance. That I am filled with all I need...that I am so incredibly blessed to have lived at all....to have loved at all (please see this incredibly beautiful you tube video.....google "you tube grateful tony moss lyric video."...(a picture of moon rays flowing over water over rocks-and press little box in corner to expand to full screen (thank you Aminata, Dr. Amanda Kemp). For sure.... even if we barely have food clothing shelter...we can still choose to be grateful.....i know easy for me to say...when I have so much privilege..... however....some of the happiest people I've met in my life....had very little money and material things....yet.... lots and lots of ....Love. So we will talk about love some more a little later (as bell hooks explains in her 'All About Love' gem of a book).**

~

<u>**Some more unhealthy macho disease values.......**</u> **(especially present with our wealthy white hetero one percenters who run the show...and have run the show from jump....however can certainly be front and center with all of us....even if we don't have a pot to piss in.... since it's all relative......and I can be a flaming ass hole with billions....or a dirt poor, flaming asshole.....as macho is alive and well across all boundaries.....and**

the price tag can literally be threat of death to any who oppose or "threaten" any of these macho "values".....which I would offer......really "de-values" the macho's... as well as those who are perpetrated against)......

competition to be # 1.. at all costs...no matter who we need to walk over to get there......

superiority.....thinking I'm better than others....because I have "won", have more etc.....

elitism.....not only am I superior.....I'm ..the elite of the elite.....on a pedestal....like the penis monument.

entitlement......since I'm better than....I am entitled to more than..
all those who are less than..ie., less"educated", poorer than, from another country etc., etc.,

and finally....

success........here's one for you.....what the hell is success?......the thing is....I can be successful at something...i.e, making money, a particular task etc......
…........guess the real question for me is....
…..........am I successful at being a "good" human being?........

~

Healthy Values Intro.

…..….which brings us to a sampling of "<u>healthy</u>" <u>other values </u> to choose to live by...(healthy...meaning they support us in <u>continually growing into better and better versions of our most loving selves</u>.............and again...what we "need" to be teaching and modeling for our young ones....and <u>the most important mission</u> and <u>core function</u> of our families, schools, churches, government, businesses, ... all our "institutions".... is to provide a foundation which reinforces these healthy core values.........(please see the "All Life is Sacred" Proposal later on).....

….and the accomplishments, accumulations...etc.,etc... are all gravy.....but not the determinant of our worth, happiness, success, serenity, etc......

The following was used as part of a keynote presentation on "Men and Multicultural Counseling". The belief is that, as we support our boys and men, and all of us, to embrace and live by our most healthy human values, racism will eventually die out.

Values

It's About Values
And Taking A Stand

This being human,
Always a <u>choice</u>.
When to take a stand,
and lend our voice.

<u>Knowing </u>our values
Being firm and clear,
Always a choice,
between love and fear.

So let's see now....

<u>"Unhealthy"</u>,

   <u>traditional</u>,
<u>masculine</u>,
   <u>values:</u>

competition
  elitism
entitlement
  superiority
power
  wealth
success
  control

Or,

<u>"Healthy",</u>
  <u>traditional,</u>
<u>feminine,</u>
  <u>(and "healthy",</u>
<u>male,</u>
  <u>values:</u>

cooperation
  sharing
generosity
  consideration
nurturance
  kindness
support
  encouragement

And,

"<u>Healthy</u>",
   <u>traditional</u>
<u>human</u>,
   <u>values</u>:

integrity
   dependability
courage
   humility
gentleness
   strength
service
   respect
equity
   patience
compassion.

Alright now...
hope that helps you some
always important to figure
where we're coming from.

Moral Inventory and Valuing Process

The following inventory was developed by my brother Glenn and adapted by me with his permission. Glenn is a caring teacher and writer about resilience and healing from trauma - please check out his books and workbooks. The idea here is to take a fair and non-critical look at our character strengths / values, first looking at how we treat ourselves, and then how we treat others. The number 1-10 serves as a guide to what improvements we may wish to make. In general, the valuing process is as follows:

Clarifying and understanding, the meaning and implications of each value.

Choosing, after carefully considering alternatives and consequences of living each value.

Taking action, which consistently reflects chosen values.

(Two other versions of this inventory (for leaders and institutions) appear as part of the All Life is Sacred Proposal, later on in this book).

The Fearless, Searching, Kind Moral Inventory*

No person can be truly at peace with himself if he does not live up to his moral capacity - Norman Cousins**

Character Strength	Rate Yourself from 1-10. 10 means you are living this strength as well as a person can.		Describe a time in the past when you demonstrated this strength		Describe what you could do to demonstrate this strength better and more often.	
	Self	Others	Self	Others	Self	Others
Courage means persisting in doing the right thing despite the pressure to do otherwise.						
Honesty means you speak only the truth, always. No "white lies," half-truths (truth can be tactful and kind), cheating or stealing.						
Integrity means your behaviors match your values and that you show your sincere, authentic self without pretense.						
Respect means you honor people and treat them as worthwhile; are civil and courteous.						
Fairness means you play by the rules, do not take dishonorable advantage of others, and treat others impartially.						
Loyalty, faithfulness, and trustworthiness means you keep commitments and confidences, don't speak ill of others behind their backs; reliable.						
Responsible means able and willing to respond to valid needs and duties; dependable; protects self and others.						
Kind, caring means you are concerned for the welfare of others, desire to help and support their growth; considerate, generous, tenderhearted.						
Sexual integrity means sexual expression is used in the context of love and concern for the other, and never used in a selfish or exploitive way.						
Tolerant means you are patient with differences and imperfections of others; forgiving						

***Reprinted from Schiraldi, G. R. (2011), *The Complete Guide to Resilience: Why It Matters; How to Build and Maintain It.* Ashburn, VA: Resilience Training International. © 2011 Glenn R. Schiraldi, Ph.D.**

Values Meditation and Prayer

May we each continually choose to break free from the chains of macho-ism which dehumanizes us all.

May we each continually choose to live by our most beautiful loving values.

May we always to our best "to listen to that little, still voice of truth inside, which gently guides us home again, to re-member, to re-connect with, our grandest version of our greatest vision of who we truly are."

~

(With deep appreciation to Neale Donald Walsch and his 'Conversations With God' books).

Neale teaches us, that **when we are facing a quandary, dilemma, painful, or scary decision, etc...we have simply to quite our minds..and ask ourselves the simple (yet likely the greatest) question we can ever ask ourselves..... "What would love do now?"...."What would be the most loving thing I can do for myself?"**

That little voice of truth will always provide the answer....we will know it is true....however we might not want to hear it...because the loving path is not always the easiest...and takes lots of courage. Yet, we can be assured, it will always end up being in our best interest.

And in the best interest of the others...even though they will often not like it because they are not getting their way. However, it will also end up being in their best interest too.

Some other less obvious forms of macho.

Patriarchy....government......of the fathers, by the fathers, for the fathers.......macho......nuff said.

And …

Patriotism / Nationalism...especially more extreme forms of both. Like sometimes...almost fanatical ..."in your face"...."USA..USA"... "we are **Better Than.. You**.....rather than ....we're all in this together.....more of a one world concept.

This is important and can get a little confusing. As it would seem like being proud of our country would be a good thing. And it is to a point. However, it can also clearly get over the top...especially when we look down on other countries / peoples.

The competition thing again..#1..at all costs..no matter..how disrespectful..."in your face"...

…....rather than...being the best we can Be.

Again....feeling proud...and grateful....for Being ... a good person....a good people.....in how we treat ourselves and All others....now that's the ticket.

What follows are two related poems that I hope you will find helpful....as re-membering the truth...can keep us humble....and help us to appreciate, value, and re-claim the best in each of us.....and All of us.

God's Anointed Ones

God's Anointed Ones
Think our leaders got it wrong.
Permission to steal and kill,
is what it meant to be strong.

A foundation built on lies,
values out of whack,
have to figure out how,
to get back on track.

One thing is for certain
we can never all be free,
til we acknowledge the truth,
and make it right, for you and me.

For the history of this land
demands we tell the story,
of what really happened,
not the pretense of glory.

If we keep speaking truth,
look each other in the eye,
connect with love and trust,
solid ground, you and I.

FRS/ 10/2/19

I Have A Dream*

-That we men, especially us white, heterosexual men,** will commit to uncovering all vestiges of white supremacy inside ourselves and this culture, not out of guilt or fear, but out of love and compassion, and justice

-That we men will start choosing Love over Fear in all our decision making

-That we men will <u>demand of ourselves</u> to stop hurting ourselves and others

-That we men will work on our own insecurity, so we will stop putting down others because they're Native, or Black, or Muslim, or Asian, or Gay, or just different

-That we men will stop being bullies with verbal, and physical threats or intimidation

-That we men will stop Choosing To Be out of control with alcohol and other drugs

-That we men will stop beating up other men to prove our masculinity

-That we men will stop raping drunk or drugged women, or any women

-That we men <u>will</u> support each other in standing up and speaking out against racism, sexual assault, sexism and homophobia

-That we men will commit to learning how to express our anger in healthy, non-violent ways

-That we men will seek help to heal the pain of our childhoods

-That we men will choose to carry ourselves with respect and dignity all the time

-That we men will be courageous enough and strong enough to be gentle and kind with ourselves and all others

-That we men will hold ourselves accountable for all of our thoughts, words and behaviors, all of the time

-That we men will remember that the real truth, happiness and serenity lies within
-That we men will choose, <u>right now</u>- to learn to love and nurture <u>ourselves,</u> physically, mentally, emotionally, spiritually, and socially, and make <u>this</u> our way of life

-That we men of VFP*** will lovingly support Women, especially BIPOC Women, in leading our organization out of white supremacy patriarchy to true equity and justice for all and lastly

-That we men will choose to have fun, <u>lots of fun</u> – without hurting ourselves or others

Roberto Schiraldi

(This poem was originally part of a panel discussion on preventing sexual assault)

*(From book, "Healing Love Poems for *white supremacy culture*", 2nd edition, to be released late fall 2021).

**(Since we are the ones primarily responsible for perpetrating the vast majority of violence in the U.S., since the beginning)

*** This version of the poem was written for the Veteran's For Peace Newsletter.

More on Trauma.

...Gabor Mate reminds us that there are many excruciating causes of trauma.....rape, incest, physical and emotional abuse, racism, sexism and all the other attacks on us from the outside......and yet **the greatest human trauma** is the excruciating disability of **being alienated from ourselves.** In his powerful, and moving tv video **'The Wisdom of Trauma'** he demonstrates how the painful lives of so many are ruined through violence, addictions, and many other life threatening behaviors....all due to the lack of intimate loving connection and acceptance of our self. Which many of us learned from day one.

So it has to start with the belief in... and sense of ....oneness... with our own precious self. And with that deep appreciation and acceptance of self....we can then choose our beautiful connection with others.

Back to Prelude Two

Real strength....going inside...looking at our self with impeccable integrity...holding ourselves accountable..... acknowledging when we fall short....amends....plan...change behavior....

Gentleness...being kind...tender hearted with ourselves and others....offering our tender hearts....to the tender hearts in all others.......as a consistent return "home" to our purest selves.

Vulnerability, the antidote to machoism

Since the time
of our ancestors,
the cave "men",
we males learned
to view everything
with **suspicion**,
hatred
and **fear**...
keeping the softness
of love
buried
deep inside,
protected
in suits of armor
and wealth.

We've all
been duped...
to be alienated...
from ourselves...
and each other.

To see ourselves
and each other
as **threats**...

instead of
as supportive,
compassionate,
nurturing,

beings
of light
and love,

Beings
who are
trust worthy.

This Original Fear
of all others
is the foundation
of racism,
and all the other
"isms",
and intentionally
prohibited
"We The People"
from ever
truly meaning
"All the People"....
never really
intended

to apply to
women,
children,
sexual orientations,
refugees,
races,
ethnicities,
abilities,
classes,
animals,
the land.

The good news!
We now have
the opportunity
to truly "evolve",
by embracing
our true wisdom,
and strength,
to be gentle,
and kind,
and brave enough,
to be openhearted,
and vulnerable..
to feel deep love.

This willingness..
to risk..
being hurt,
is the essence
of real growth,
real love,
real men,
healthy humans.

Vulnerability and Strength.

Let's be clear. <u>Vulnerability</u> as we are discussing it here.... is <u>_not_ about weakness, or being taking advantage of, or running from bullies, or allowing ourselves or those we care about...to be intimidated, hurt, etc.....especially from those using their racism, sexism, homophobia, transphobia, classism, xenophobia, or any other excuses to dis-respect others.</u>

I have had some men of color respond negatively to my talk of vulnerability. "Yeah, easy for you to say, you don't have to be worried about being profiled". Or, "There is no way I'd teach my son to be "vulnerable", in a society that already treats us like second class citizens."

From my previous book on 'Men and Racism,' some stories that follow to help clarify.

Story #1.

One of my respected and trusted racial justice allies and friend spoke out in a meeting about his anger at how protective he felt for the safety of his son, especially if he might be stopped by police. This is a fear he felt was very common to most Black parents. As a Black man of slave ancestors... and someone who had personally been subjected to racial profiling..... he was understandably very concerned and protective of his son especially regarding any possible interactions with police. So he continually took extra care in supporting his son, and reminding him to treat all others with respect...... <u>to stand up for himself... intercede when others were being bullied,....not take crap from anyone</u>.....yet to be very very respectful with any interactions that might occur, with those in authority...especially police. This included specifics like, keeping hands on the wheel in a traffic stop, "yes officer, no officer", complying with requests respectfully, etc.

Story #2.

I was offering a training for staff of a local outpatient alcohol and other drug treatment center on how male issues were related to alcohol and other drug use/abuse/addiction. One of the staff, a single parent, spoke of how, while she agreed with some of what I was saying about the importance of teaching and modeling for her sons healthy and respectful emotional expression....she was extra concerned about her sons being hurt and taken advantage of if they were perceived as "vulnerable" or weak. I expressed support and understanding for her concerns, and added...." this is about teaching to them to be strong, be able to take care of themselves, and stick up for others, when appropriate....... and also to be confident enough in themselves,and their values that they are willing to be humble, sensitive, kind, gentle...etc...the highest qualities that would allow them to be their fullest selves. Strong and Gentle. Brave and Kind."

Story #3.

A wonderful father of two young Black boys from another country, spoke to me about his challenges, in raising two <u>strong, honest, brave</u>, young men.....yet with the highest priority being.....them not losing their inner "<u>soft hearts</u>" in reaction to a world which was often a "<u>hard</u>" place. Again, a seeming dilemna. ... and / or..an opportunity to model strength and gentleness as complementary....and on the road to real freedom and empowerment.

To <u>choose</u> to Be <u>vulnerable</u> is this <u>amazing courageous conviction</u>...which allows us to fully experience our greatest strengths.....of being our most beautiful authentic self.....and to being able to open our hearts.... our lives....to others .....and to give and receive the most precious gift of all.....Love. A risk, to be sure....since opening to love always brings with it the risk of deep, deep pain.

<u>Story #4, My Love Eileen.</u>

A little over a year ago my Beloved Eileen passed after a long bout with cancer. The grief has been excruciating. The sadness, the tears, sometimes felt never ending. Yet I'm slowly coming out again....and I wouldn't trade it for anything.

She is still very much alive inside me, and always will be.

So before we committed to each other.....we were walking, hand in hand, as we often did, along the Tow Path next, to the Canal.....when ...Love and Fear collided inside me..... and I collapsed crying on the ground. Eileen kneeled down and held me...gently asking...."What's wrong Roberto?" When I was able to collect myself....I shared with her, what I had never done with anyone else in my life (and I had been married, and had a step child, twice before)..... that I was scared to death/life of losing her. If she drove back to Phily and got killed in an "accident"...I would be devastated...and didn't know if I could go on. That's when I knew...undeniably...felt it ...to the deepest core of me....... LOVE ....and the FEAR....of BEING ....VULNERABLE...... YET WITH THE CERTAIN KNOWLEDGE THAT I HAD GIVEN MYSELF THE GREATEST GIFT IN THE WORLD......LOVE..... Choosing to lovingly face the fear and risk of losing her...and the love we co-created,by our mutual spiritual commitment to ourselves and each other.....was and will always be....my single greatest accomplishment.

Was I and were We...perfect? Hell / Heaven ...NO!.... There was a lot of rough going....especially since I am such an imperfect human.. with many, many imperfections.

However, as they say.....we were and are perfect together....because we did our best to honor our commitments to the ingredients of Love, (again, more about the ingredients of Love, from bell hooks and her book 'All About Love' later in the All Life Is Sacred section.)

And when we fell short, because we are both very human...we did our best to prevent any drama..... and to acknowledge and understand what happened, what our plan to change was, and do our best to carry through. One of our many great gifts together. From choosing to commit to ourselves and each other...through the FEAR of Being Vulnerable to Love.

As a wise one reminded me...."the depth of the pain is a reflection of the depth of the love". Yet with the pain....I have so much joy and gratitude....feeling like the most blessed man on the planet....that this incredible human being chose to love and accept me completely for who I am...with all my goodness, and all my imperfections. I am a better human, and better able to Love and appreciate all the wonder of this life. So I smile and laugh when I think of her...and sometimes I feel sad and cry....and I welcome and honor all of those feelings...that are.. and will always Be.. Alive In Me.

Fear of Tears.... or......Honoring Our Tears.....A Truly Radical Path to Healing

What are we so afraid of?.......we'll be called a baby...wimp..... weak....a girl ... and on and on. We'll just be a puddle of tears.... and never get out of it to be strong..... or we'll just be giving in to our weakness, and never do what we need to do to protect ourselves from all the threats out there......or is it really ...in here..in us. "I'm not afraid of my tears....I don't feel any." Yikes....that's sad...and maybe more that a little scary. While it may sound contradictory.....I have gratefully learned...that a major part of happy lives, and healthy emotional balance .... can be our connection to, and celebration of, our tears (which, of course, can also be tears of joy).

So when we wall off from our tears....we learn to hide behind a suit of armor...to protect ourselves from being "vulnerable"...to all the other "threats in our lives".....we cut ourselves off <u>from ourselves</u>, and deprive ourselves of one of the most important, powerful, and <u>essential</u> aspects or our hu<u>man</u>ity ...of Being a healthy, emotionally balanced, <u>real</u> man (real men Do cry)..... And again, in his powerful video, 'The Wisdom of Trauma', Gabor Mate teaches us, the greatest trauma is the trauma of being alienated from ourselves. And stuffing tears....deffinitelydishonors....and alienates us from ourselves.

Often times we don't even allow ourselves to cry at funerals... Be A Man....Be A Man......that is totally insane. Crying is how we _honor_ our feelings, and how we grieve to heal our great losses. Yet we are often taught to "survive" without this amazing, life affirming...... soothing.... comforting...... nurturing......cleansing........ freeing.....healing.....gift......... crying........honoring and then releasing deep sadness and grief.....which is about as natural and _free_ as we can get.... (along with of course, great joy.. another part of being truly alive and "thriving").

So many of us men, are emotional basket cases, due to our tenuous hold on our emotions. So we strive to be stoic robots....(yet are allowed to bully with anger...or even act out in rage)....and we wonder why we have racism....and violence against women children, animals, the planet.... and ....war!

When we tend to our natural inner need to cry, we are also able to be much more happy and emotionally well-balanced After some great and tender cries....we can feel ....soothing relief.....cleared out....maybe even ready to start letting go of old losses, wounds, and fears that no longer serve us..... We can make healthy loving decisions... followed by healthy loving action....perhaps by asking ourselves...."What would love do now?" This doesn't mean we won't still grieve some pain and losses, maybe for the rest of our lives. It does however, mean we can also decide to savor the sweet memories and feelings, heal and appreciate who we are, and what we have now, and in the future.

<u>My fear of crying governed half of my life</u>. I'm convinced that my absolute terror at being found out to be less than.... unworthy.....not smart enough...not good enough.....liar.... cheat...fraud...weak...a coward.....were the fears that drove so many of my decisions and actions for at least half of my life. Finally in my mid forties, after being suicidal, I got into recovery and decided that if I was going to choose to live...... I would need to make a life long <u>commitment</u> to learn about real love, and how to really respect, honor and love myself and others, by living in complete integrity,and by facing all of my fears....especially of being vulnerable. So I started doing some deep grief work, allowing myself to cry, which I hadn't since early childhood (to be a man), along with deep rage work (i.e., yelling at the top of my lungs, beating cushions etc, however being fully committed to not hurting myself or anyone else with it (didn't need more self-inflicted hurt)). As part of my self care routines, I'd set times aside, when I wouldn't be interrupted, and would have some time to rest after (sometimes I would actually feel energized afterwards). Along with meditation, prayer, and journaling, little by little I finally started feeling free of the deep dark block of granite hurt in my gut, and started actually liking myself.....and not so afraid of being vulnerable ….actually seeing it as a path to being the man I truly wanted to be.

Now, when I see something, or read, or hear a song, or am out it nature and some sensation, or sad memory or thought comes up, and I allow myself to cry....I feel so grateful.... so Gratefull. (Again, if you haven't already, please listen to and see the beautiful and moving Grateful....by googling "you tube grateful tony moss *lyric* *video*" (and click on the little box in the corner for full screen view).

And when I see a movie, or re-member
some beautiful story....and I laugh, and I cry, and experience many other feelings......I really know I'm getting my "money's worth."

Years ago there was an amazing love song I heard....(wish I could find it)....it basically said....**the greatest gift I can give you....is the gift of my tears.** Makes me re-member... **some of the moments when I have felt closest to another human being was when we held each other and shared our tears.** And yet, unfortunately, those moments have been all too few. For me, this is real emotional intimacy... where real trust and safety and love can flourish. Ideally, of course, it is part of an ever growing commitment to core ingredients of love......like gentleness, integrity, courage, humility, dependability, kindness, compassion....... Some wise one said...."Each tear is a another drop of healing".

This book on macho.....can be most complemented by a companion guide on the essence of healthy crying...which might just be my next one. Or maybe one of you will decide to write it. In the meantime, for more inspiration about the gift of our tears, please see the work of Henri Nouwin, 'Men and Grief', Richard Rohr, 'The Gift of Tears', Dr. Kate Truitt, 'Keep Breathing', and my Dear Friend Dr. Amanda Aminata Kemp with Dr. Sina Smith ('Why is Crying Good'/'Why is Fall the perfect time to grieve', on you tube video),

My Sacred Feminine

Alive
In me
Is the
Miracle
Of Life.
Continually
Being reborn
Renewing
Recreating
Nurturing
Sustaining
Energy.
Compassionate
Soothing
Comfort.
Forgiving
Humility.
Healing
The wounds
Deep
To the core
Of Mother Earth
Of me.

A gentle
Salve
Washing over
The scars.
Joyfully
Pronouncing
Freedom.

FRS/12/06

The following is an outline for a proposed organization in support of men coming together to support each other in learning, growing, healing, to become better men, and support our boys in becoming healthy men, in service of a better world.

Men for Racial Healing and Justice Proposal

Men for Racial Healing and Justice is an organization of men who are concerned about addressing racial healing and justice for ourselves and the world around us. While we males have made and continue to make so many positive contributions to our world, we are also, unfortunately, responsible for contributing to the vast majority of violence, oppression and destruction.

We believe that effective racial healing and justice must begin with us men holding ourselves and each other accountable and standing together to insist on racial healing and justice for us all. Safe, supportive environments are provided in which to do this most challenging and often painful work. With the support of other safe, strong, caring men, together we can heal ourselves and the world.

Our mission is to continue to deepen our understanding of the white heterosexual male supremacy value system /

how it has hurt us and our common humanity, and pitted us against ourselves and each other. This is the underlying, belief which drives our efforts. Fearlessly speaking this truth with love and action is our commitment.

Advocacy/Consultation/Individual and small group support

Providing individual and group support for stepping up and speaking out about racial justice. Exploring efforts to effectively interact with individuals and systems. Providing support for healing from racial trauma, and other related concerns.

Programs

A variety of programs are designed for organizations and institutions to explore the roots of internal and external racism and the ways to change ourselves and the world in ending racism.

Two Day - Four Day Intensive Gatherings. " The Many Myths of Being Male: The Keys to Ending Racism".

These programs will allow for in-depth internal work and creating relational and team building opportunities as we peel away the lies that have oppressed us and hurt our common humanity. We will come away feeling refreshed and invigorated in our commitment to healing ourselves and ending racism.

Spiritual Healing Ceremony

Meditation and prayer circles

Sweat Lodges

Drumming Circles

Embracing the Quiet Within

Learning how to be compassionate with ourselves, each other, and our Earth Mother.

Program topics to include:

Growing up male

Stereotypes /gender role conditioning

Competition to be #1 at all costs (no matter who you need to walk over)

Power, wealth, control

Macho / bullying

Real strength / Gentleness

Fear of Women (based on book by Wolfgang Lederer)

Fear of Being Vulnerable / The Importance of (Safely) Honoring Our

Emotions

Healthy Life Balance

Healthy Relationships

Healthy Sexuality

Archetypes - warrior, hero, king, lover...

Fatherhood

Friendship/Brotherhood

Celebrating Maleness

Being Impeccable With Our Word

Our Sacred Path

Our Sacred Nature

*LOVE, what it really means, how racism is the lack of love, and how real love for ourselves and all life, is the antidote.

A Poem on the Reassuring Principle of Balance.....

PERFECT BALANCE

SEE SAW OF LIFE

FULCRUM

CONTRAST

ALL AS IT NEEDS TO BE

<u>ALL</u> <u>IS</u> <u>WELL</u>

THE BALANCE OF LIFE
HEALS OUR STRIFE

FRONT BACK

IN   OUT

UP   DOWN

ALL   AROUND

DARKNESS LIGHT

ASLEEP   AWAKE

FEAR   LOVE

HATRED LOVE

WAR   PEACE

TOLERANCE ACCEPTANCE

SADNESS   JOY

COMPAINING GRATITUDE

PAIN   RELIEF

DIS-EASE   EASE

CRITICIZE AFFIRM

~

ALL HAVE

ELEMENTS OF

THE OTHER.

THUS..

THE PERFECT BALANCE

SEE SAW OF LIFE

FULCRUM

CONTRAST

ALL AS IT NEEDS TO BE

<u>ALL</u> <u>IS</u> <u>WELL</u>

ALWAYS HAS BEEN

ALWAYS WILL BE.

~

WITH ALL
ITS WARTS

THE UNIVERSE
IS MIRACULOUS.

WILL I
CHOOSE
TO
FULLY ACCEPT
AND EMBRACE
AND BE GRATEFUL
FOR IT ALL?....

THAT IS THE
QUESTION.

AND CONTINUE
TO DO MY PART
TO HELP PROMOTE

HEALING....

AND LET GO
OF THE REST
THAT I CANNOT
CONTROL.

SO I CAN BE
PEACEFUL
AND
JOYFUL
AND
REST.
SO I CAN
HELP
RECREATE
ANEW....

AND SO
IT GOES

AND SO
IT IS.

BIRTH LIFE DEATH REBIRTH

CIRCLE OF LIFE.

Another poem on Balance...to remind us....that sometimes ...in fact... most likely always......the most challenging...people, and events.... can provide the greatest insight and implications for healing....and Loving Action.

The bully balance

So many bullies

racist

sexist

homophobic

classist

nationalist

familial

relational

work place

and on and on and on.....

again....

finding the balance here

is key.

So many opportunities...

to learn and grow from.

When and how

do I stand up

to the bullies?

Sometimes

I need to pause

and breathe in

and envision

a good way

to handle

the situation.

Having faith..

that Higher Power

and

goodness

and

love

are always

in me.

It can be

very difficult.

Especially

when the anger

or fear

rises up.

Thus

stepping away..

and

the loving

soothing,

comforting...

reassuring...

breath.

Sometimes

finding the way

to connect

with the bully...

To hear

and feel

what is real

in their heart

and mind...

Sometimes

choosing

to address it ...

another day.....

another way....

Sometimes....

choosing

to stand

and fight.....

I've rarely
felt good
about
turning away......

wasn't being a man.

And yet.....
maybe
wouldn't have

made it
to 79..
if I hadn't.

And now...
picking battles.....
and doing
my best
to be accepting...
compassionate....
loving......

is way
more important......

however....
the prickles of …..
coward....
fear.....
not standing up
for what's right.....
will always
move me
to action......

the goal being.....
loving....
healing....
mending......
action.

So....
each bully.....
is a gift....
to awaken me ….
to be alert.....
to be fully present.........

to look at the bully …..
deep in their eyes........
in their hearts........
even just for a moment...
in time....

and maybe
that connection....
that recognition
of them....

is really
what they

have been
longing for
all along.....

doesn't mean
it will always work....

for folk's pain
runs deep....

fueling all
the horrific
"isms",
oppression
and trauma.

And
I can be
the bully...
to myself......
to my love ones....

By controlling,

criticizing,

being insensitive,

and unappreciative..

on and on......

So....

I will
continue
to Be Committed

to Be
and Do
My Best

to address
the bullies

inside me ..

and others....

as the universe
brings them
on my path.

~~

May you

choose

to do the same....

and may we all help

each other

on this amazing

racial justice journey.

P.S. If our leaders are bullies....then we may need to take a strong stand for equity and justice for All. And we will need strong allies to do so.

*What If Washington Was Gay?

<u>(of course, given what has come before...this would need to be healthy...non-macho gay)</u>

**None of what follows is issued as a put down.
It is offered as a perspective to consider....
In our efforts at healing.**

It's what I see as the core element, rarely discussed, that just might contain the cause / healing for our challenges with racism, sexism, militarism.... macho-ism.. and on and on.

<u>*What If Washington Was Gay?</u>

What would the implications Be

for ourselves...

for the government...

for all institutions.....

for the Veterans for Peace Board...

and for our Stance

against Militarism

and

Sexism

and

Racism?

How might our fear of being Gay

be similar to

our fear of being Racist?

How does all the above

relate to

wealthy white hetero male supremacy

cultural values?

~ ~ ~

**The Problem
As I See It.**

Being straight
is the way
anti gay.
all the way.

Since day one
macho man
suit of armor
rusted can.

Afraid of weak
safety we seek.
protection our task
so we wear a mask.

<u>Alienation from ourself</u>
put our <u>feelings</u> on the shelf....
put our <u>feelings</u> on the shelf
<u>alienatation from ourself.</u>

Only one way out
by going all in
acknowledging our fears
releasing our tears.

Honoring our feelings
finally bridges the gap
being true selves
we finally beat the rap

Of being hard as nails
chasing our tails
Distant at best

Everything a test.

Finally we can breathe
Finally....we....can....breathe
and go back to the start
as we live from our heart.

* (Or what if Washington was a Woman?..... (I have for so long hoped for a BIPOC woman for president).....although as I've often said....it wouldn't really matter if she was a Poor Immigrant Trans Latina....if she was still emulating the same ...macho values....then....nothing really changes.)

And one more piece on balance......

<u>GAY</u>   <u>STRAIGHT</u> ·   <u>CONTINUUM</u>

FLAMING HETERO ON ONE SIDE ////////////////////////////
FLAMING GAY ON THE OTHER

MOST OF US......SOMEWHERE IN BETWEEN.

SO WHAT'S THE BIG DEAL?

AND FOR THOSE OF US
WHO LIvE ON ONE END OF THE SPECTRUM
OR THE OTHER.....

COOL!

AS LONG AS WE DON'T
SIT IN JUDGEMENT
OR IMPOSE OURSELVES
ON ANYONE ELSE.

EACH OF US
FREE TO BE
OUR TRUEST SELVES..
WITHOUT FEAR OF BEING PUT DOWN.

EACH A VALUABLE PART
OF THE
BEAUTIFUL TAPESTRY OF LIFE.

This proposal is offered, with hope that all those in power (including you and me), will consider going back to the beginning, to boldly, lovingly, recreate a new vision for ourselves and each other. A Loving Vision of the Sacred... for Healing America...and our world. I offer you this, with hope and faith in our individual and collective commitment to living our lives with full love....Being all we truly can be.

ALL LIFE IS SACRED

A Loving Blueprint
For Healing America

" I am poor and naked, but I am the chief of the nation. We do not want riches, but we do want to teach our children well. Riches would do us no good. We could not take them with us to the other world. We do not want riches. We want peace and love"

-Red Cloud (Makhipiya)
(late 19 century) Lakota Chief

Introduction: The Original Core Values

To Review:......While our Constitution espoused positive sounding values of liberty and justice for "All The People"... Women and Native People were excluded from the document, and African American males were counted as 3/5th of a person. Beautiful values and guiding principles of Love - honesty, fairness, kindness, compassion, generosity, respect.... were largely forgotten in the desperate quest for power, wealth and domination.

So in actuality, at it's core, the U.S.'s founding values were more indicative of fear, greed, hatred, material wealth, power and control, which further devolved to elitism, entitlement, superiority. "Success", was equated to competing to be #1, at all costs, no matter who we need to walk over to get there. Those initial values were derived by the misguided principles of "doctrine of discovery" by "god's anointed ones", justifying "manifest destiny". Those principles resulted in the genocide of the Indigenous People, the original inhabitants and stewards of the land, and the horrific inter-generational treatment of enslaved Africans upon whose backs our country's economy was largely built. Additionally, the careless slaughter of the animals and desecration of the land....all for the use of those in power.

The aforementioned paved the way for protecting those in power by establishing and justifying institutional core values of racism, sexism, homophobia, classism, xenophobia, ableism, ageism and on and on. So yes, we have many blessings, and of course, we also have many severe problems. So that's the quick and very dirty, explanation for the state of affairs we find ourselves in.

Now.....what do we do about it?

Choosing New Core Values To Live By:

All Life Is Sacred

Again, as I see it...the answer is really quite simple....and yet.... profoundly challenging. We each choose to claim, and live by, the incredibly powerful, core, loving principle......."All Life Is Sacred"....Sacred...meaning worthwhile, important, valuable, precious, worthy of love, respect, dignity, awe and wonder. This also translates into this new perspective that I'm no better, no worse than that insect, the Land, that tree, that Woman, that child.....**ALL Life Is Sacred.** Once we live by the love principle, all of the poisonous "isms" would die out. The sacred inter-connectedness of all life...takes center stage..... we literally live by the idea of **"All interconnected, All One"**. This has always been a core spiritual principle. Now, the science of quantum mechanics demonstrates that at a cellular and molecular level, all of our cells and molecules are always changing and intersecting with all others. So we literally are, all connected and all one.

From the Lakota Native Spiritual Tradition...Mitakuye Oyasin (pronounced – mee tock o yay – o yah sin), meaning "All My Relatives, All My Relations, "We Are All Related... All One"...Each One my Sister, Each One my Brother....The Animals Are My Relatives...The Trees....All part of the Sacred Circle Of Life, The Sacred Hoop...Mother Earth, Father Sky, Grandfather Rocks, Wind Spirits, Thunder Beings....all Guides and Teachers from the Great Beyond.... All To Be Honored and Cherished...and All to live with in Harmony. So I do my best to Be Grateful for the Sacred Gift Of Life, and for all the Gifts...My Relatives....and choose to release differences and judgments of myself and all others.

> *"Lose all differentiation between myself and others, fit to serve others I will be.*
> *And when in serving others I win success, then will I meet the Buddha.. and we will smile"*
>
> *-Milarepa, The Great Yogi of Tibet*

So if this was the core guiding principle which drives the purpose, the vision and mission statements of every school and church, and all the other institutions in our country... and the world...imagine...please imagine....the affect and effect on all of our children, and their children's children for the next seven generations to come......We will treat ourselves and each other with utmost gentleness, kindness honesty, respect, fairness. Because we are all in this together...we do not see anyone as an adversary in competition for a little piece of the pie. There is plenty to go around for everyone to have a high quality of life, when we choose to live with utmost mutual regard for the sacredness of all beings.

This is a system of values which is in **everyone's** best interest...individually and collectively. Of course, this would require a full-on **agreement**....and full-on **commitment...** by everyone. A **100% commitment** to being our best, with complete honesty and compassion in every thought, word and action, in how we treat ourselves and each other. A high bar to live by ….to be sure. And yet.....we would have soooo much to gain....every one of us. And living by this guiding principle of the sacredness of all life creates this incredible opportunity for "**Loving** Thy Neighbor **As Thyself**". That's it. As simple as I can put it.

So now, a little more about this thing called **Love**.

Love

Since the beginning, all the wise ones have said …..Love **Is** the answer.

So, what is this elusive butterfly called Love?

As the inimitable Tina Turner sang...*"What's Love Got To Do With It?"***.......the answer......Everything!**
The most powerful force in the universe is LOVE! Always has been, always will be. We humans just forget. And to be fair, it's mostly because we haven't really been taught about love......not nearly as we need to be. The word is thrown around so carelessly, most often without really even knowing what we mean by it. ***"It's just a feeling....can't really be explained....but you know it when you feel it"***......**like that. Talk about bogus. We've been brainwashed, bamboozled, hoodwinked.......to desperately seek this ….thing......that**

we can't even describe......and we wonder why so many relationships with ourselves and each other end up not feeling fulfilled. <u>As the wise and courageous activist and writer bell hooks (lower case, her preference) so heart-fully teaches us in her wonderful book "All About Love".....we need to define the core values of love (my words, not hers), and then we can create lives filled with those values. Values like gentleness, kindness, commitment, integrity, courage, vulnerability, dependability, fairness, compassion, understanding, responsibility, respect, gratitude, trust, and being willing to support ourselves and each other in our mutual spiritual growth. Spiritual growth, for me, implies a life-long learning adventure in deepening my inter-connectedness with all other life, so that we may best serve all others.</u>

So we're not talking about mamby pamby, goo-goo, ga-ga fantasy love, we're talking about the real deal....fierce, active, passionate, clear, on solid ground LOVE. And it has to start with us being taught about how to honor, and cherish, respect, and care for **ourselves**. And holding ourselves to the highest and most honorable standards of human decency and fairness. If we are willing to bravely venture into this adventure in learning how to love ourselves....and to share that with others as we grow......which,to me, is the main purpose for our being born,.....then all good things are possible.

So there you have it sports fans! That, to me, is the essence to our living harmoniously with ourselves and each other, on our Sacred Mother Earth. The question then becomes...if we agree, in principle about the aforementioned core values of the sacredness of all life, and of living in love as the blueprint for honoring the sacred....then what are we willing to do about it?

For me it's all about the powerful word...... "COMMITMENT". Am I....Are You....Are We....each individually...and collectively......ready.....willing.....and able to commit to living our lives in beauty...walking the Sacred path of Love....in all of our thoughts, words and actions........... ...individually and collectively? If we are....we can fix the problems we've co-created..... if we are not.....then we will continue to have the unfulfilling existence we have. Again, commitment, to me, means....100%...all in... not 99%....for that 1% will sabotage our best efforts. That doesn't mean we will do it all perfectly...that's not the point. It's that when we mess up, which we will....no big drama, no excuses..... just, pick ourselves up, dust ourselves off, look honestly and humbly at what we missed that created the misstep, acknowledge it, come up with a better strategy for fixing it expediently, and then carry through with a sustainable plan. In Twelve Step Programs we call it taking a fearless and searching moral inventory and making amends, and committing to and following through on real change. This is similar to the Truth and Conciliation process which so many individuals, families, communities, nations have used to great avail. (Please refer back to some of my prior poems and pieces on truth and conciliation if you're interested in reviewing a little bit more about these and other similar, complementary processes).

I don't know about you...but I'm ready, willing and able to commit to co-creating the amazing life
here, and around the world, that I believe we were all put here to live. I hope and pray, that you are too....and that is why you are still reading this.

~

"Out of the Indian approach to life there came a great freedom – an intense and absorbing love for nature; a respect for life; enriching faith in a Supreme Power; and principles of truth, honesty, generosity, equity, and brotherhood as a guide to relations".
— **Luther Standing Bear (1868-1939)**
Oglala Lakota chief

Real love is humble, and gentle and kind, courageous, and impeccably honest. The following are guides to live by, to create inner well-being and outer well-being for us all. So let's look at some of the core ingredients of love and what they represent, (at least to me)

And as we explore these core values more and more, it becomes clearer how they each intersect with and complement each other:

Core Love Values

Courage- The willingness to lean into the difficult challenges of life, to Be, and to Do the "right thing". Even in the midst of others' disapproval. A great guiding question for any quandary in life is...."What would love do now?" "What would be the most loving thing I can do for myself in this situation....that little still voice of truth inside, will always guide us home.....to love....if it doesn't feel right, then the guide isn't love, it's usually fear or guilt. Really important to keep re-learning about that distinction. Are we willing to be courageous enough to be vulnerable...with our feelings....this is the mark of a true love warrior.

Honesty- A strong promise to ourselves to act and speak with authenticity. No white lies. When we "get over" on others we're really getting over on ourselves. No way we can feel good about ourselves without living honestly. "The truth **will** set us free". Which is why it is so essential to live by this core value. Lest we be imprisoned by our secrets. "We are as sick as our secrets" (from 12 Step Principles).

Integrity- Living with a strong sense of justice and fairness. We live congruently....our behaviors match our values. And again, a willingness to speak up and take action when we see or feel inequity and injustice. Living with impeccable honesty and integrity frees us to live in peace with ourselves, and to feel a deep sense of respect and acceptance.

Kindness - We treat ourselves, and others with gentleness, compassion, generosity, empathy, understanding, support. Again, it is crucial that our relationship with ourselves is based on utmost kindness. Otherwise our treatment of others, will likely fall short, and ring hollow, eventually, even leading to resentment and sabotage. Are thoughts and actions reflect our desire for the well-being of ourselves and all others.

Commitment - We consistently follow through on our promises to ourselves and others, especially when the going gets tough. And with all these, when we fall short, no big drama, no beating ourselves up, compassionately acknowledging where we went wrong, and revising strategies that are perhaps more realistic and more sustainable.

Dependability - We do what we say, and say what we do. Similar to integrity. We believe and have faith in ourselves, because we carry through on our commitments...first and foremost with ourselves, and of course also with others.

Responsibility - We take pride in being accountable to ourselves, first and foremost...honoring our most important love priorities in self-care, and the care of others. Being responsible for our well-being fills us with a sense of contentment and peace, since we know we are "taking care of business". Having clear boundaries is very important. If we don't know what our limits are, and don't honor them, we can become resentful, and being doing things out of guilt and fear, not love.

Fairness/Equity/Equality – We treat ourselves and others with a sense of fairness, equity and justice. We do our best to ensure equal and fair access to life necessities for all, economically.. food, clothing, shelter, educationally, healthcare...a desirable quality of life for all. If one of us is suffering, it hurts our common humanity. Again, there is plenty to go around if we live by fair and just standards.

Patience and Acceptance – We do our best in all of our thoughts words and actions to be very patient with our imperfections, and to hold ourselves and others with unconditional positive regard. We do our best to check our judgments of ourselves, to treat ourselves fairly. And we strive to do the same with others, by trying to put ourselves in their shoes. While this can be extremely difficult....like with all of these values, it can also be extremely rewarding, as it gives the best chance of interconnecting with others who may seem different than us.

Trust - Trust takes time to build for ourselves and others. When we consistently demonstrate over time, that we are trustworthy, that is true to our word, then trust becomes a great gift we give ourselves and others. When trust is broken, this is how we determine our willingness to recommit to our core principles. We can do this by carefully accessing what let to the break in trust,and what needs to happen to regain the trust for ourselves and the other. A sincere, heartfelt amends, when appropriate can be very helpful. And then following through on well-thought out strategies to make things right for ourselves and with others (ideally,vetted by the injured party). And of course, consistently carrying through on our commitments to change, and monitored over time. If need be, reassessing and altering strategies as needed.

Respect – Treating ourselves and others in the way we would like to be treated. Being respectful and considerate of our and others' feelings, and needs, as consistent with our core values of love and sacredness of all life. Respecting all boundaries, especially sexual ones. Treating ourselves and each other with dignity and reverence for each one's worth. This can be especially difficult when there is significant disagreement, Yet, most disagreements can come to fair and equitable resolution, if both parties are committed to treating each other with respect and kindness, and a willingness to meet in the place of equity and fairness.

Gratitude/Affection – Wise elders often say that gratitude is one of the most important love values there is, and can be a true source of genuine affection which we all so greatly need. Affirming and acknowledging our self care, along with our gratitude to the other, can be beautiful and heart filling gifts which make a huge impact on our mental, emotional, spiritual, physical and social well-being.
And relationships individually and collectively can prosper and grow through this simple act of loving expression.

Spiritual Growth - Willingness to nurture spiritual growth in self and others - When we choose to believe in and live by a belief in the core worth of ourselves and others, and of our inter-connectedness to all things, then our life becomes a reflection of that core value, by how we treat ourselves and each other in our daily lives. Decision making about the most simple, and the most difficult challenges becomes more achievable as our confidence grows through the experience of our spiritual growth.

<u>Core Love Values Inventories</u>

Using the Core Love Values Listed Above, please consider filling out the following two Core Love Values Inventories For Self and Others, and for Leaders, Institutions and Organizations. For the second inventory, you might start out by picking one leader, institution or organization that moves you to want to take action, and see what comes up for you. (Institutions and organizations may include any groups such as schools (especially teaching accurate history), healthcare,wildlife, environment, churches, business, police/prisons (of course would include treatment of inmates), military, government (especially promoting truth and conciliation processes), and others. In service of all the people, all leaders, institutions and organizations would optimally be reviewed internally and externally (perhaps by unbiased, carefully selected, civilian review boards) for realistic compliance and sustainability on an annual or bi-annual basis. And, for example, a mailer could be sent to cross sections of the state populations or townships asking for feedback using the inventories for whichever leaders institutions/organizations are up for review. Feedback could then be summarized and used for regular review and planning sessions. Citizen ownership would then be a vital, ongoing, mutually advantageous process. Data from both inventories help us determine what is working, and improving what needs improving. This is not about being adversarial with ourselves or others, it's about working together for optimal outcomes for all.

<u>All Citizen's Core Love Values Inventory For Self and Others*</u>

Core Value	Rate how treat self/others from 1-10(10 being optimal) Self/Others		Describe recent time demonstrated that value Self / Others		Describe specific plan to improve that value Self / Others	
Courage						
Honesty						
Integrity						
Kindness						
Commitment						
Dependability						
Responsibility						
Fairness/Equity Equality						
Patience/ Acceptance						
Trust						
Respect						
Gratitude/ Affection						
Cooperation/ Service/Sharing						
Spiritual Growth						

Based on Fearless and Searching, Kind Moral Inventory from Schiraldi, G. R. (2011), *The Complete Guide to Resilience: Why It Matters; How to Build and Maintain It*. Ashburn, VA: Resilience Training International. © 2011 Glenn R. Schiraldi, Ph.D. Not to be reproduced without written permission* *Human Options*. Toronto: George J. McLeod Limited, 1981, p. 45.

<u>All Citizens' Core Love Values Inventory For Leaders, Institutions, Organizations*</u>

Core Value	Rate how leader treats employees and public from 1-10 (10 being optimal)		Rate how Inst./Org. treats employe/pub. (from 1-10)		Describe recent time demonstrated that value		Describe specific plan to improve that value	
	Emp	Pub	Emp	Pub	Leader	Inst./Org.	Lead.	Inst./Org.
Courage								
Honesty								
Integrity								
Kindness								
Commitment								
Dependability								
Responsibility								
Fairness/Equity Equality								
Patience/ Acceptance								
Trust								
Respect								
Gratitude/ Affection								
Cooperation/ Serv./Sharing								
Spirit.Growth								

Tree Of Living Love

The following is a visual representation of the Tree Of Living Love – a symbol of the mutual commitment to live and nurture ourselves and each other... All life. One way to view this is to envision a truth and conciliation process, that is, speaking the truth about our history, and seeing it all, through the eyes of a gardener and the garden of life. We live in a beautiful garden. There are many gorgeous flowers and plants of all colors and shapes. There are also invasive and aggressive weeds that may look attractive, however, left unattended, may drain the soil of it's nutrients, and overpower and suffocate the natural healthy and balanced growth of all of the flowers and plants. It may be noted, that the poison of some of the weeds, blended with the sweet pollen of some of the flowers and plants, can have powerful healing properties. So the gardeners need to first learn about and recognize the poisonous roots of decay. And then the garden needs continuous, vigilant weeding and tilling and revitalizing of the soil to maintain the precious life affirming balance.

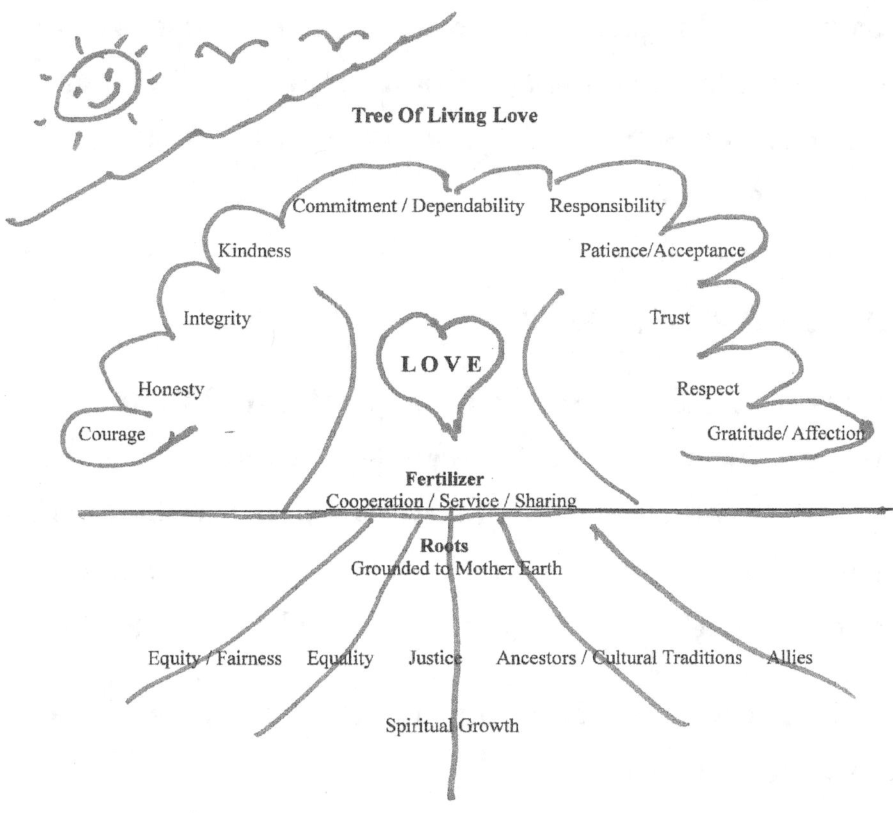

Tree Of Living Love
Commitment / Dependability   Responsibility
Kindness   Patience/Acceptance
Integrity   Trust
LOVE
Honesty   Respect
Courage   Gratitude/ Affection
Fertilizer
Cooperation / Service / Sharing
Roots
Grounded to Mother Earth
Equity / Fairness   Equality   Justice   Ancestors / Cultural Traditions   Allies
Spiritual Growth

Commitment Proposal

It is proposed, that every citizen will sign and commit to live by the following agreement(whether born here or not... refugee, immigrant, young, old, gay, straight, parent, child, blue color worker, white color worker, educator, government servant, police/peace keeper, business person,...and on and on)....in other words, everyone of us.

All Citizens' Agreement*

I, as a citizen of this Country, of this World, as a representative of ...All The People....Pledge my life, to do my best with every thought, word and action... to make choices based on the core belief that All Life Is Sacred, and that each choice will reflect core Love values by:

1. Checking and accessing my commitment with each core value as listed

2. Expressing each value commitment out loud to myself, and ideally to another I feel responsible to

3. Continuing to reassess my commitment of my pledge to myself and the others I serve, through regularly scheduled written and spoken self-reflection

4. Committing to maintain regularly scheduled, mutually agreed upon reviews with those I serve

5. Signing my name as my promise to live by each value

This is my word.

Signed

**(It is recommended that a yearly day of celebration be initiated to honor every citizen's living by their sacred pledge).*

The Creator, Great Spirit, Wakantanka, The Universal One, never fails to remind me of the sacred, loving path, and the ongoing work to restore balance.

- My cherished teacher of the Lakota traditions, Tom/Rags sent two beautiful passages to me about the importance of the two-spirited ones (who embody the greatest qualities of the sacred feminine and sacred masculine, all in one), and who are beautiful, healing empaths for us to turn to for wisdom, healing, guidance.

- Another grueling, agonizing pipeline protest by brave Indigenous People and their supporters, to prevent further illegal desecration of sacred lands.

-My beloved friend and brother John invited me to accompany him in support of some distinguished Lakota Elders who are part of a delegation traveling east to retrieve the remains of Lakota children who died at one of the first Indian boarding schools. The children had been forced to leave their families and tribes (to be "assimilated", "kill the Indian, save the man"), often treated horrifically, many never seeing their loved ones again. Their families and tribes had been previously prevented from taking their remains home. Now, over a hundred years later, they can be brought home. The wounds so deep...so deep. Yet, finally, maybe now, their spirits can be free. And a little healing can start.

*For a moment....if you would.....please take a deep breath...
close your eyes... and try to imagine how you would feel...
in your heart and body.... if one of these children.... is your
child.*

The Children

Oh... the Children.
their spirits
yearning to be free.

Finally they can return
home again
to their loved ones.

And their spirits
can continue
on their sacred journey.

Honoring Our Children
…..from the plantations
…..from the boarding schools
…..in the border detention centers
…..in human trafficking
All of our children, everywhere
For seven generations to come.

All children want to know..
Am I loved?
Will I be comforted?
Is the world safe?

The answers determine
a kinder world.

In saving our children,
We save our country.

In saving our children,
We save our world.

In saving our children,
We save...ourselves.

Honoring the children
through loving action
is how we can re-create
a loving world.

Mitakuye Oyasin
All My Relatives

Please keep the spirits of the young ones, who have suffered
so much, in your loving hearts and prayers ..... their families
and loved ones, ... the elders who continue this difficult
healing work.... and all those who work to make it right.

Parting Considerations

~

"When the first chakra is disconnected from the feminine Earth, we can feel orphaned and motherless. We look for security from material things. Individuality prevails over relationships, and selfish drives triumph over family, social and global responsibility. The more separated we become from the Earth, the more hostile we become to the feminine. We disown our passion, our creativity, and our sexuality. Eventually, the Earth itself becomes a baneful place. I remember being told by a medicine woman in the Amazon, "Do you know why they are really cutting down the rain forest? Because it is wet and dark and tangled and feminine"
\- Alberto Villoldo, Ph.D,
Dance of the Four Winds: Secrets of the Inca Medicine Wheel.
(With loving appreciation, to my dear friend and colleague Dr. Maria del Carmen Rodriguez, for sending the above quote to me, and for her loving help with with this work.)

~

Please see <u>"America Needs A Woman President", by Brett Bevill, drawings by Eben Dodd,</u> a wise and moving little book which really gets to the heart of our huge need for more Women in leadership positions, especially Black, Indigenous, LGBTQ2S, and Women of Color, who live and lead by the core sacred love values previously discussed.

~

"I am going to venture that the man who sat on the ground in his tipi meditating on life and its meaning, accepting the kinship of all creatures, and acknowledging unity with the universe of things, was infusing into his being the true essence of civilization."

— Luther Standing Bear (1868?-1939)

Oglala Lakota chief.

The following mediation prayers are part of my daily ritual:

Mediation Prayer To Stop War

May All People Everywhere

Stop The Wars

Within Us

And

With Others.

And May We

Fill The Void..

With

LOVE.

Meditation and Prayer For Compassion and Kindness

May All Of Us

Find Compassion and Kindness

Within...

And Give It to Ourselves...

And All Others.

Meditation and Prayer For My Mind and Brain Stuff

(Breathing In and Out Slowly..

May My Mind
Be Peaceful and Calm...

May All My Brain Stuff
Be Soothed and Comforted...

In This Moment
I Breathe In Deeply...
And All Is Well...

I Release
All Sense of Fear.. and All Sense of Urgency

In This Moment

I Have No Where To Go
Nothing To Do

But Be Here Now..
In This Precious Moment

All Is Well..
I Am Safe and Peaceful

I Savor This Precious Moment..
I Savor This Precious Breath.

Mediation Prayer For My Authentic, Loving Self.

May I Walk
With Dignity and Respect

May I Always
Do My Best

To Be Impeccable
With My Word

And To Have Every
Thought,
Word,
and
Action

Be A Reflection
Of My Most Loving Self.

Closing

Through Macho and Beyond

So that's what I have to offer you...at least for now.

May you each celebrate the beautiful, authenticity of you and your tender heart....now and for all your future breaths of your loving life.

Additional Author Information

Dr. Roberto Schiraldi, EdD, LCP, LCADC is a licensed professional counselor, licensed clinical alcohol and other drug counselor, and has been a racial justice advocate, trainer, and trauma therapist for over 40 years. Roberto is retired from Counseling and Psychological Services at Princeton University, where he was coordinator of the alcohol and other drug treatment team, and was previously employed in a similar capacity by Temple University, where he received his doctorate in Holistic Health Education and Counseling. He is a past President of the New Jersey Association for Multicultural Counseling, past Co-Chair of the Ethics Committee of the New Jersey Counseling Association, and has been a member of numerous racial justice organizations, boards, and committees. He is a pipe carrier in the Sicangu Lakota Native Spiritual Healing Tradition, a Vietnam era veteran, and member of Veterans For Peace.

~

***To contact me**, please go to my website www.robertoschiraldi. com, (with related racial justice podcast interviews, and information on how to order my other books, and two abridged audio books, both recorded in my voice (each approx. two hours long), one on 'Healing Love Poems for white supremacy culture', and the most recent one, on 'Post Traumatic Macho Disorder: The Way Home').*